# INTRODUCTION

This book is designed for any teacher who has a desire to introduce his/her students to the Spanish language in a fun and exciting way. Neither the teacher nor the students need to have any previous language experience. Pronunciations are given clearly and adapted easily.

The book is broken down into 13 different units of study. Each unit begins with an English/Spanish vocabulary list that will introduce the teacher to the vocabulary that will be taught within that unit. Each units concludes with cue cards that are printed with the Spanish vocabulary on one side and the English translation on the reverse. These cards can be cut out and put into an index file for quick reference.

In each of the units you will also find Fun Sheets. These sheets are to provide the students with a miniature study book of their own. The sheets should be saved until all the units are completed and then made into a book that the students can share with others or review for themselves.

By using a hands-on, experiential approach for introducing a foreign language, young children will quickly begin using their "new" vocabulary words in their day to day activities.

# Table of Contents

# UNIT 1

# DAYS OF THE WEEK

## VOCABULARY

|  |  | (pronunciation) |
|---|---|---|
| Monday | lunes | loo-nehs |
| Tuesday | martes | mahr-tehs |
| Wednesday | miércoles | myehr-koh-lehs |
| Thursday | jueves | ghweh-vehs |
| Friday | viernes | byehr-nehs |
| Saturday | sábado | sah-bah-doe |
| Sunday | domingo | doh-mihn-go |

# DAYS OF THE WEEK

Incorporating the Spanish translation of the days of the week into your regular curriculum can be done many ways. One very simple method is to alter your room calendar slightly. By attaching cue cards with the Spanish words for the appropriate day of the week, children find a new dimension to the classroom calendar. As children become familiar with the new Spanish vocabulary, encourage them to recite the words before revealing the cue card's English equivalent.

## CALENDAR GAMES

Games are another enjoyable way to integrate the Spanish days of the week into the curriculum. Collect some cardboard pieces and using a permanent marker write down the new Spanish vocabulary. Punch holes into either ends of the cardboard and attach a string through the holes; this makes it possible for children to wear the word. Divide the class into groups of eight children. Have seven of the children wear the seven Spanish days of the week. The remaining child must try to align the children in the correct order and then recite (in Spanish) the days of the week. For added fun, have relays or timed races. This game is recommended for children who already have a fairly developed understanding of the new vocabulary.

# SONGS TO REINFORCE

Any music already existing with English lyrics can be used by replacing with the new Spanish vocabulary. Children can make patterns of beats for the days of the week as well. Let one child clap the beats of the syllables in the word "lunes." Then let the next child clap the syllables in the word "martes." Continue the process until every child has had a chance to clap the beats of at least one day of the week. This way all of the children have experienced the pronunciation of the new vocabulary words in slow repetition.

# DAYS OF THE WEEK
# FUN SHEET

Using the space provided in the right hand column, draw a picture of the things that you would like to do on any given day of the week. The left column indicates the day that you would participate in that activity. Be prepared to share your ideas with your friends using the new Spanish vocabulary for the days of the week.

| | |
|---|---|
| **LUNES** | |
| **MARTES** | |
| **MIÉRCOLES** | |
| **JUEVES** | |
| **VIERNES** | |
| **SÁBADO** | |
| **DOMINGO** | |

# UNIT 2

# MONTHS OF THE YEAR

## VOCABULARY

|  |  | (pronunciation) |
|---|---|---|
| January | enero | *eh-nehr-oh* |
| February | febrero | *feh-brehr-oh* |
| March | marzo | *mahr-so* |
| April | abril | *ah-bril* |
| May | mayo | *my-yo* |
| June | junio | *ghoo-nee-yo* |
| July | julio | *ghoo-lee-yo* |
| August | agosto | *ah-go-stoh* |
| September | septiembre | *sehp-tee-yehm-breh* |
| October | octubre | *ohk-too-breh* |
| November | noviembre | *no-byem-breh* |
| December | diciembre | *dee-syehm-breh* |
| Autumn | el otoño | *el oh-toh-nyo* |
| Winter | el invierno | *el een-byehr-no* |
| Spring | la primavera | *lah pree-mah-beh-ra* |
| Summer | el verano | *el beh-rah-no* |

# MONTHS OF THE YEAR CALENDAR

Like the vocabulary for the days of the week, the new Spanish vocabulary for the months of the year can also be integrated into your regular curriculum. Using two loose-leaf book rings, construct your own "rolodex" of cue cards containing the spelling and pronunciation of all twelve months in English and Spanish. Place this rolodex near the room calendar and use it for recitation and for the game described below. Laminating the cue cards will preserve them for future years.

## BIRTHDAY GAME

If you keep a birthday calendar in your room, add some Spanish flavor by playing the Birthday Game. Children love celebrating their special day of the year. Have them tell you their birth month using the new Spanish vocabulary in this unit. If you have children who may be too young to recall the month they were born, come prepared to class with those dates. Begin by reciting the months of the year in Spanish slowly. When the children hear their month they stand until the next month is introduced. Pick up speed as you go through the months a second and third time. Children love the movement and speed so be prepared for some volume! Variations might include having the children clap, sit, or if you are really brave, have them shout back the month when it is called.

# SEASONS

Divide the class of children into four equal groups. Set up work stations in four different areas of your classroom. Assign each group to a work station. Explain to the children that each work station represents one of the four seasons. Label each "seasonal" station with the Spanish name for that season.

Send the groups to their particular seasonal station. At their station the children should discuss the activities and weather conditions that are special to that season. Upon completion of the discussion the children, (as a group) should paint a picture of their assigned season. When the seasonal picture is completed, each group will have the opportunity to present their seasonal picture to the rest of the class.

Have each of the children use the following sentence to begin their description of their painting and tell about the activities of that season that they like.

**En**
(ehn)

**el otoño**
**el invierno**
**la primavera**
**el verano**

**me gusta** _____.
I like
(may goo-stah)

(In the season I like _____.)

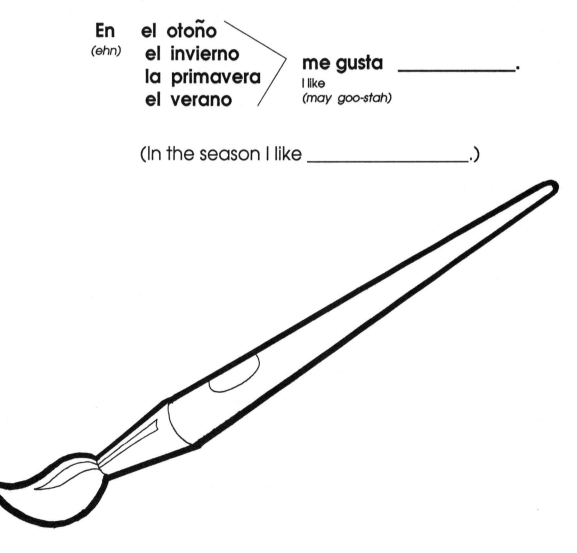

Cut out the pictures and glue them next to the month that best matches that picture.

| | |
|---|---|
| **enero** | **julio** |
| **febrero** | **agosto** |
| **marzo** | **septiembre** |
| **abril** | **octubre** |
| **mayo** | **noviembre** |
| **junio** | **diciembre** |

- - - - - - - - - - - - - - - - - - - - - - - - - - - - - - - - - - - - - -

# UNIT 3

# NUMBERS

3 4 5 1 2 8

## VOCABULARY

| | | *(pronunciation)* |
|---|---|---|
| one | uno | *oo-noh* |
| two | dos | *dose* |
| three | tres | *trehs* |
| four | cuatro | *kwah-tro* |
| five | cinco | *seen-koh* |
| six | seis | *sehs* |
| seven | siete | *syeh-teh* |
| eight | ocho | *oh-cho* |
| nine | nueve | *nweh-beh* |
| ten | diez | *dee-yes* |
| eleven | once | *ohn-say* |
| twelve | doce | *doh-say* |
| thirteen | trece | *treh-say* |
| fourteen | catorce | *kah-tor-say* |
| fifteen | quince | *keen-say* |
| sixteen | dieciséis | *dee-yeh-see-sehs* |
| seventeen | diecisiete | *dee-yeh-see-syeh-teh* |
| eighteeen | dieciocho | *dee-yeh-see-oh-cho* |
| nineteen | diecinueve | *dee-yeh-see-nweh-beh* |
| twenty | veinte | *behn-teh* |

# NUMBERS
# CALENDAR

Using your room calendar, you can teach the days of the week, the months of the year and numbers in Spanish. Children love some change in the regularity of routine. Having the children recite the numbers leading to the actual date in Spanish can be fun. For some variety, read the numbers backwards or have a child lead the recitation. You could give a title to the child leading the recitation: "Señorita/Señor Número" (Miss/Mister Number).

# NUMBER BINGO

Copy the four cards provided on the following pages so that each child in the class has at least one card. Then use paint or magic marker to label nine ping pong balls or pieces of paper with numbers 1 to 9. Use whatever you can think of for the children to mark off the numbers on their card (dots, beans, popcorn kernels, etc.). Put the squares or balls in a concealed container and proceed with the regular game of Bingo. In this game however, you can only use numbers in Spanish. Pick different children to be the number caller.

# NUMBER BINGO

| | | |
|---|---|---|
| 1 | 3 | 4 |
| 5 | 9 | 7 |
| 8 | 2 | 6 |

# NUMBER BINGO

| | | |
|---|---|---|
| 8 | 1 | 5 |
| 3 | 6 | 4 |
| 9 | 2 | 7 |

## NUMBER BINGO

| | | |
|:---:|:---:|:---:|
| 8 | 6 | 3 |
| 2 | 4 | 7 |
| 9 | 5 | 1 |

## NUMBER BINGO

| | | |
|:---:|:---:|:---:|
| 9 | 3 | 6 |
| 2 | 5 | 7 |
| 4 | 1 | 8 |

# FROG HOP GAME

This game requires advanced planning. Cut out 10 large green lily pads from felt or construction paper. With a marker or felt put a single number from 1 to 10 on each lily pad. Use the pattern included to make a frog costume. For durability felt is recommended, but paper is fine.

When lily pads and the costume are prepared you can begin the game. Have one child dress up as the frog. Tape the lily pads around the room 1 to 1 1/2 feet apart. Then instruct the child dressed as the frog to jump from lily pad to lily pad giving out the number indicated on the lily pad as he/she jumps. The number must be given in Spanish. For variation, have the frog jump and the other children shout out the numbers that the frog is jumping on. This game encourages learning through excitement and movement.

(Make 2)

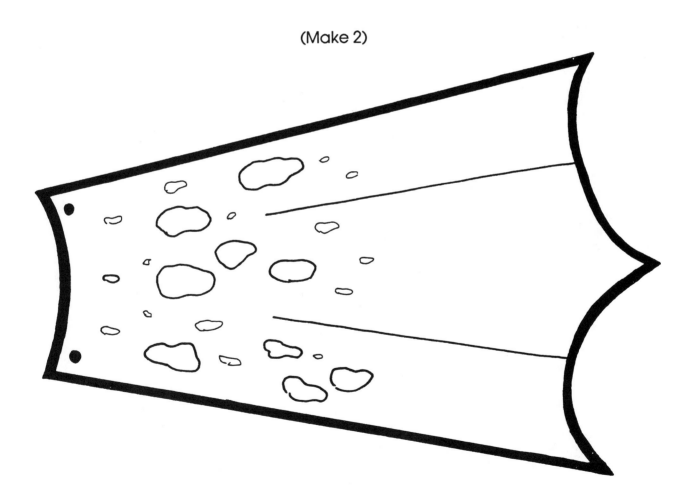

*(Punch holes and add string so frog feet can be worn by the children)*

# FROG HOP GAME

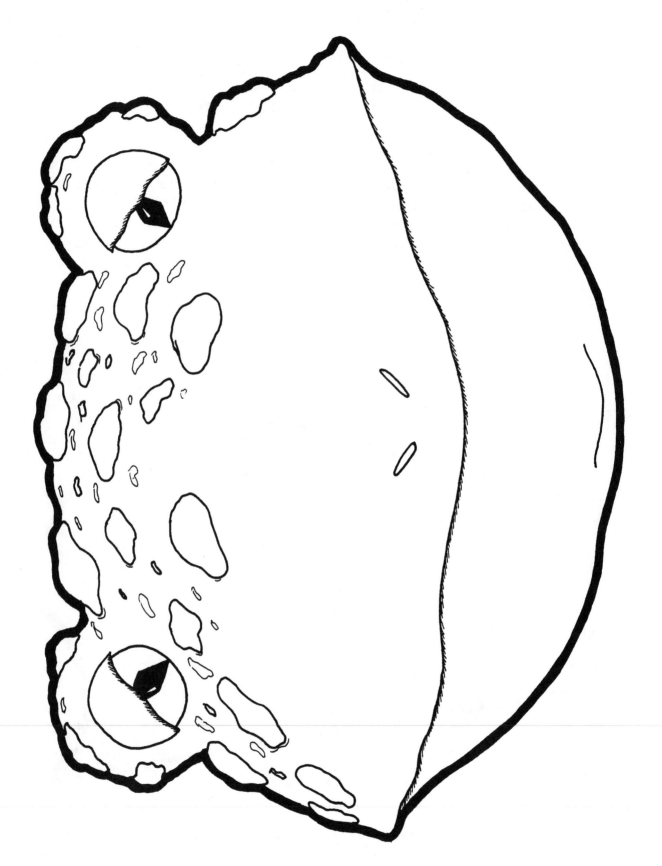

*(Punch holes and add string so the frog face can be worn as a mask.)*

# FROG HOP GAME

# THE NUMBER GAME

Copy pages 26 and 27 to create the numbers gameboard. *To begin the game:* give each child a penny to use as a marker on the gameboard. The children take turns rolling the dice. The player with the highest number on the dice goes first. *To play the game:* The children take turns rolling the dice and then moving that number of spaces on the gameboard. The children should be encouraged to say the numbers in Spanish. The player who reaches the finish line first is the winner.

**START**

**FINISH**

# MAIL BOX GAME

Collect 10 shoe boxes before beginning this game. Wrap the boxes with butcher paper carefully so that the lids are removable. Then label them from 1 to 10. Make a slit (the size of a letter envelope) in the top of each box. Attach a flag (made out of construction paper) with a brad to each box. Then label 10 letter envelopes with the numbers 1 to 10. When this is all complete you are ready to begin the game.

Place the mail boxes around the room so their numbers are clearly visible. Appoint a child to be the mail deliverer. If you can find a mail bag or large purse the game is even more interesting. Put the letters in the bag. Without peeking, have the mail person choose a letter from the bag. Then he/she must hold the letter envelope up so that all the children can give the matching Spanish mail box number. The child must then deliver the letter to the correct mailbox. Try moving the mail boxes around the room every few days.

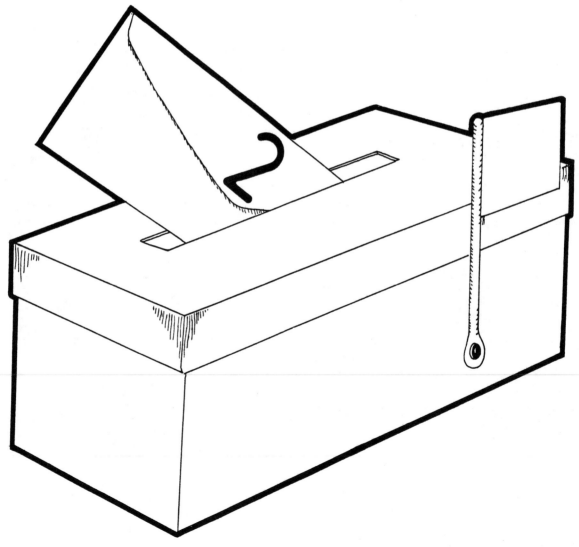

# UNIT 4

# COLORS

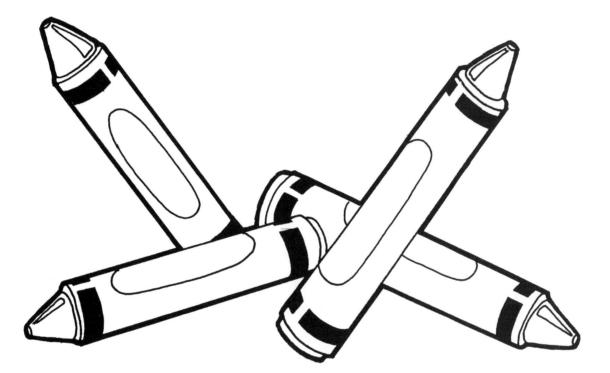

## VOCABULARY

|  |  | *(pronunciation)* |
|---|---|---|
| red | rojo/a | *roh-gho/roh-gha* |
| green | verde | *behr-deh* |
| orange | anaranjado/a | *ah-nah-rahn-ghah-doe* |
| yellow | amarillo/a | *ah-mah-ree-yo* |
| blue | azul | *ah-sool* |
| purple | morado/a | *moh-rah-doe/moh-rah-dah* |
| black | negro/a | *neh-groh/neh-grah* |
| white | blanco/a | *blahn-koh/blahn-kah* |
| pink | rosado/a | *roh-sah-doe* |
| brown | color café | *koh-<u>lore</u> kah-feh* |

# COLOR BINGO

Copy the bingo cards on pages 34 to 36, producing enough copies for each child in the class to have at least one card. Have the children shade in the appropriate color in each square (use the vocabulary at the beginning of the unit for assistance). Color and cut out the 10 circles seen on page 37 and put them in a concealed container – these will be drawn to determine what corresponding square on the card may be covered up. Use dots, beans, popcorn kernels, etc., to mark the cards when the colors are called.

Have a student act as the color caller and instruct him/her to only use the Spanish vocabulary words for the colors he/she draws from the container. Use regular Bingo rules (of 3 squares in a row) to determine the winner. The winner then should become the color caller.

| COLOR BINGO | | |
|---|---|---|
| ROJO | NEGRO | AZUL |
| ANARANJADO | AMARILLO | MORADO |
| VERDE | BLANCO | COLOR CAFÉ |

# COLOR BINGO

| | | |
|---|---|---|
| ROJO | NEGRO | AMARILLO |
| BLANCO | COLOR CAFÉ | ANARANJADO |
| AZUL | VERDE | ROSADO |

# COLOR BINGO

| | | |
|---|---|---|
| NEGRO | AZUL | ANARANJADO |
| AMARILLO | COLOR CAFÉ | VERDE |
| BLANCO | MORADO | ROJO |

# COLOR BINGO

| VERDE | MORADO | COLOR CAFÉ |
|-------|--------|-----------|
| ANARANJADO | BLANCO | NEGRO |
| AMARILLO | AZUL | ROJO |

# COLOR BINGO

| AZUL | NEGRO | AMARILLO |
|------|-------|----------|
| COLOR CAFÉ | MORADO | ROJO |
| ROSADO | VERDE | ANARANJADO |

# COLOR BINGO

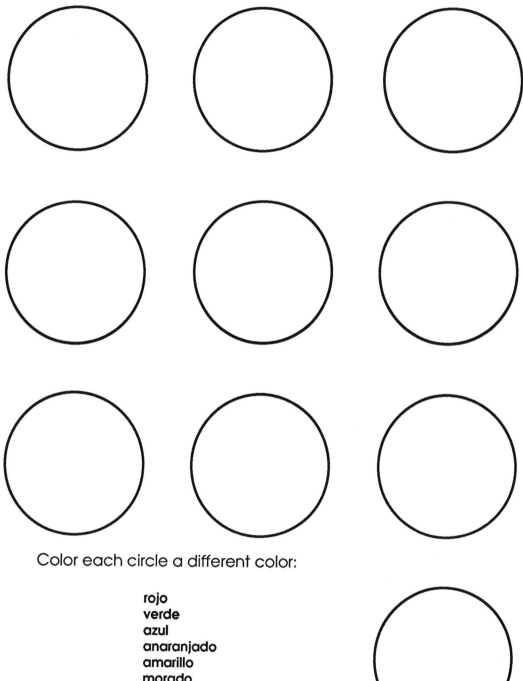

Color each circle a different color:

**rojo**
**verde**
**azul**
**anaranjado**
**amarillo**
**morado**
**negro**
**blanco**
**rosado**
**color café**

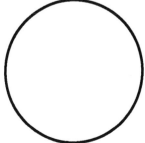

# COLOR MATCHING GAME

Copy the pattern of the bear and shirt. Make eight copies. Color the eight bears' shorts different colors (blue, red, green, yellow, white, black, orange and purple). Color the shirts with matching colors. You may wish to laminate these items and encourage children to use the game during their free time.

To begin the game, select eight children and give them each a single bear. Have them leave the room and give eight other children a single shirt. Then invite the other children holding bears to re-enter the room. Those children holding the shirts should be concealing the color of the shirt from those children holding the bears. Those holding the bears must ask children in the room if they might have a particular color shirt that would match their bears' shorts. The key is to only use Spanish vocabulary words for the colors. The child who finds the matching shirt for his bear must call out his color in Spanish and sit down before the others have found their matches.

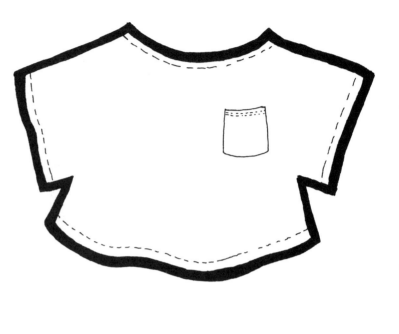

Below is a spin dial of colors with the Spanish color vocabulary labeled. Copy and glue dial to a heavier cardboard. The spinner can also be copied and glued to a heavier paper. Using a brad, attach the spinner to the center point indicated on the dial. Allow children the chance to spin the dial and take turns naming the indicated color in Spanish.

# SPIN DIAL FOR COLORS

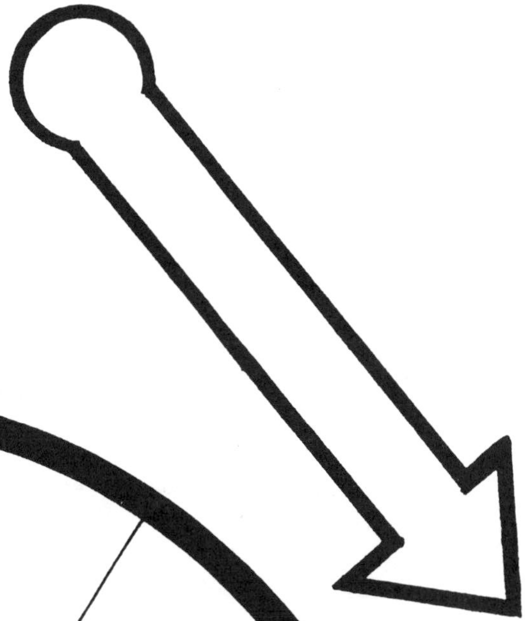

amarillo

color café

anaranjado

verde

rojo

azul

negro

morado

NAME _____

Draw a line from the colored crayon on the left to the object of the corresponding color on the right. Then, choose a friend and check each other's answers. Remember to use Spanish vocabulary in your discussions.

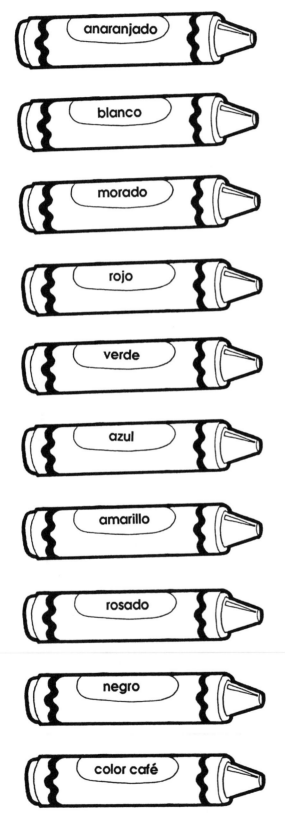

# UNIT 5

# WEATHER

## VOCABULARY

|  |  | (prounciation) |
|---|---|---|
| It's sunny | Hace sol | ah-say sohl |
| It's hot | Hace calor | ah-say kah-_lore_ |
| It's cloudy | Es nublado | ehs noo-blah-doh |
| It's cool (fresh) | Hace fresco | ah-say frehs-koh |
| It's raining | Llueve | jweh-bay |
| It's cold | Hace frío | ah-say free-yoh |
| It's snowing | Nieva | nyeh-bah |
| It's windy | Hace viento | ah-say byen-toe |
| It's bad, ugly out | Hace mal tiempo | ah-say mahl tyem-poh |
| It's beautiful | Hace buen tiempo | ah-say bwehn tyem-poh |

# WEATHER PATTERNS

Use the patterns below to cut felt shapes for various weather conditions. They can be used on a felt board or they could become a part of the room's decor. If left at an appropriate height in the room, children can use the patterns during their free time. Children must always employ their Spanish vocabulary when using this material. These patterns can also be used for the *News Bulletin Game* described on the next page.

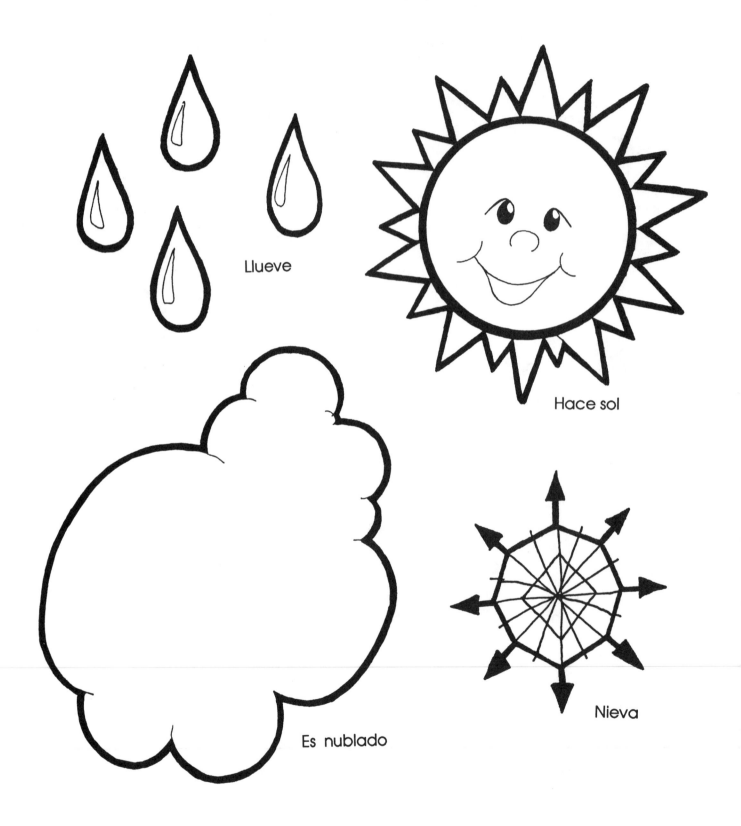

Llueve

Hace sol

Es nublado

Nieva

# NEWS BULLETIN FOR WEATHER

Keeping a daily weather bulletin in the classroom is helpful in strengthening Spanish vocabulary in this area. Use a large piece of bristol board and write the following short sentences in large letters . . .

Today is _____, el_____ de_____ de_____.
           *day*              *date*        *month*      *year*

The weather is _____.
                     *what weather **looks** like*

The temperature is _____.
                       *what weather **feels** like*

In the blank spots place the day of the week, the date, the month and the year. This can be done in Spanish or English depending on the unit your are working on and the comprehension level of the children. Place the type of weather in the next blank. This can be done with Spanish words or weather pattern cut-outs (see page 44). Be certain the children are using their new vocabulary terms to describe the day. The temperature blanks can be filled with any of the three main temperatures...Hace fresco, Hace frío, or Hace calor. Doing this exercise everyday is enjoyable and the repetition will become part of long term memory storage. As the children progress with their Spanish, have them fill all the blanks with Spanish vocabulary.

Below are three thermometers. Each has a different Spanish phrase below it telling how hot or cold it is outside. You can show the mercury levels in the thermometers by coloring them red to the correct levels.

**Hace fresco**          **Hace frío**          **Hace calor**

Color the different weather patterns. Take some time to discuss the types of weather with your friend. Remember to use your new Spanish vocabulary for weather and temperatures.

# UNIT 6
# PARTS
# OF THE BODY

## VOCABULARY

| | | (pronunciation) |
|---|---|---|
| ears | las orejas | *lahs oh-reh-ghahs* |
| mouth | la boca | *lah boh-kah* |
| nose | la nariz | *lah nah-rees* |
| eyes | los ojos | *lohs oh-ghohs* |
| shoulders | los hombros | *lohs ohm-brohs* |
| arms | los brazos | *lohs brah-sohs* |
| hands | las manos | *lahs ma-nohs* |
| legs | las piernas | *lahs pyehr-nahs* |
| knees | las rodillas | *lahs roh-dee-lyahs* |
| feet | los pies | *lohs pyehs* |
| hair | el pelo | *el peh-low* |

## PARTS OF THE BODY

"Simón Dice" ("Simon Says") is a time-less game children love. Try using the Spanish Body Parts vocabulary to play "Simón Dice" (See-mohn Dee-say). Initially, as children are first getting acquainted with his/her own body parts, they will be watching and learn-ing both visually and auditorally. Eventually advance to having the leader give the directions without any visual clues. Finally, take turns allowing children to play the role of Simón.

## HEAD AND SHOULDERS, KNEES AND TOES SONG

"Head And Shoulders, Knees And Toes" is a song most children are fa-miliar with. Start by singing the song slowly and gradually speed up the pace. Watch the children have a great time with this Spanish variation of this old song.

## CABEZA, HOMBROS, RODILLAS Y PIES

Cabeza, hombros, rodillas y pies,
cabeza, hombros, rodillas y pies,
    Rodillas y pies (repite)
Tengo dos ojos, una nariz, una boca
    y dos orejas.
Cabeza, hombros, rodillas y pies,
    rodillas y pies.

# SEÑOR AMARILLO– PARTS OF THE BODY

Señor Amarillo (Mister Yellow) is easily adapted into any classroom environment. Not only do the children enjoy using him as a Spanish learning tool during group times but he is also enjoyed during play time in which children use him in game formats.

Señor Amarillo's objective is to teach children basic body parts in an enjoyable way. Using the cut-out patterns found on pages 53 to 55, Señor Amarillo can be cut out of felt or construction paper. Have children take turns adding parts to his body and identifying each part in English and Spanish until Señor Amarillo's body is complete. *(Note: Señor Amarillo's main body parts should be cut from yellow paper or felt to help reinforce the Spanish colors. If cutting Señor Amarillo from construction paper, laminating the parts is advised. This allows for greater child participation during free play and a greater longevity of Señor Amarillo.)*

The body parts of Señor Amarillo may be labeled on one side to help reinforce the new Spanish terms as children are being introduced to this vocabulary. As they progress, try using the reverse side without any labels to construct Señor Amarillo.

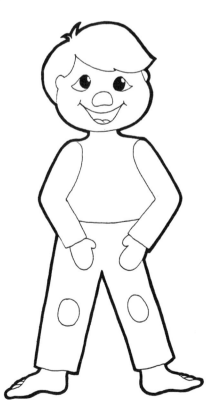

# THE BODY PARTS OF "SEÑOR AMARILLO"

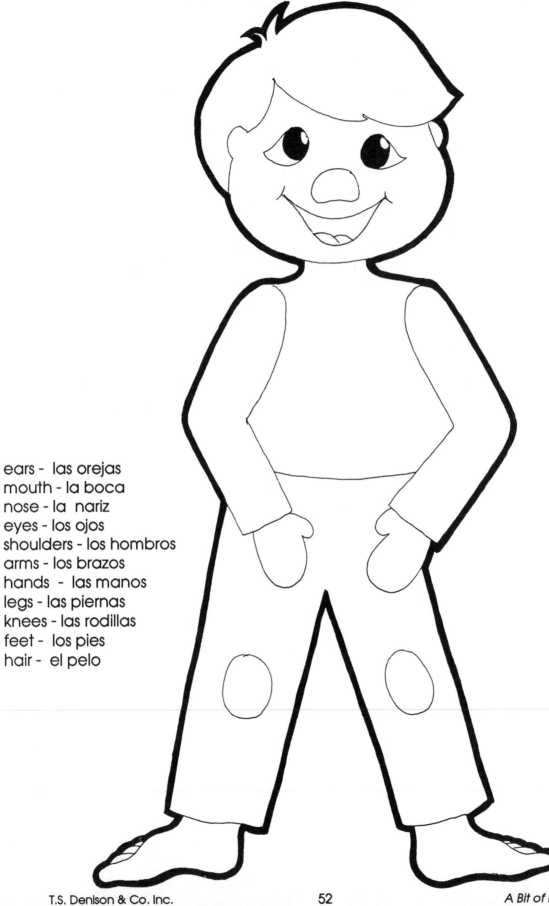

ears - las orejas
mouth - la boca
nose - la  nariz
eyes - los ojos
shoulders - los hombros
arms - los brazos
hands  - las manos
legs - las piernas
knees - las rodillas
feet -  los pies
hair - el pelo

# SEÑOR AMARILLO PATTERNS

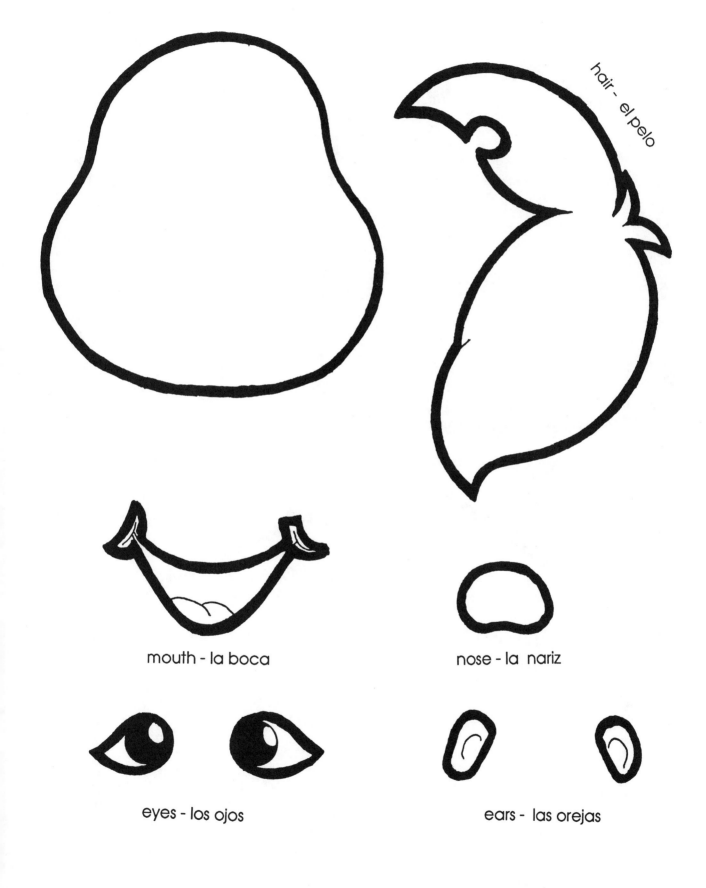

hair - el pelo

mouth - la boca

nose - la nariz

eyes - los ojos

ears - las orejas

# SEÑOR AMARILLO PATTERNS

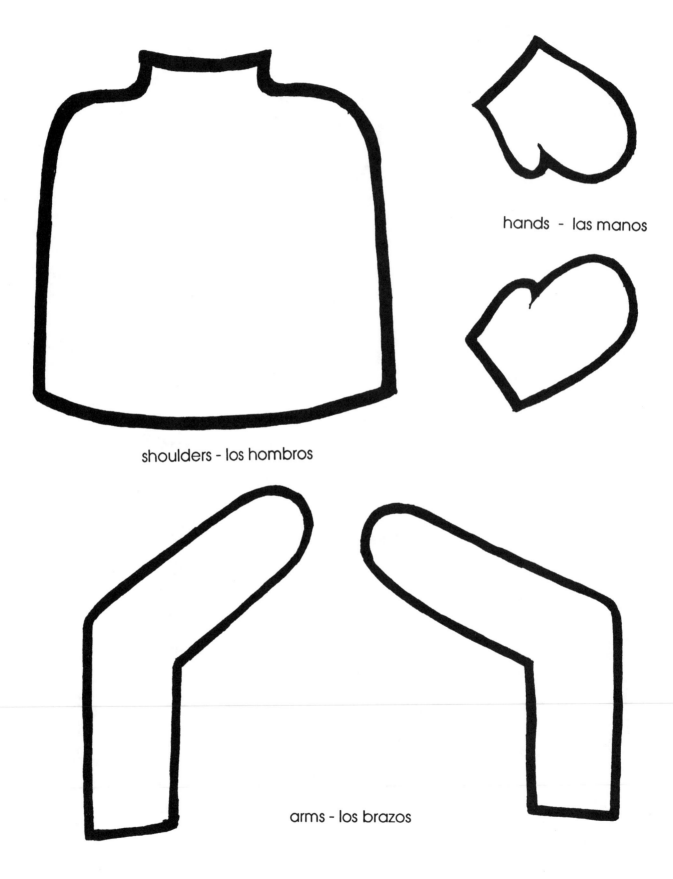

hands - las manos

shoulders - los hombros

arms - los brazos

feet - los pies

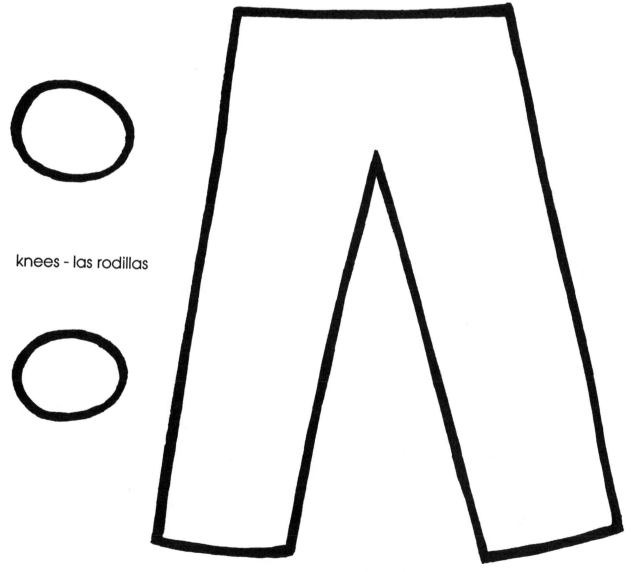

knees - las rodillas

legs - las piernas

# SPIN DIAL GAME

Use the pattern below to make a spin dial. Use a brad to attach the arrow. To make the dial more sturdy the pattern could be attached to a heavier cardboard stock and/or laminated. Then, cut out the flashcards for the appropriate unit of body parts. Have children take turns spinning the dial and choosing a flash card. Children should make up an action corresponding to their Spanish body part flashcard and repeat it as many times as the dial indicates.

*Example:* A child chooses "cabeza" for the Spanish vocabulary word and spins the number 3 on the spin dial. The child might tell the other children to touch their head three times, or roll their heads three times.

*Note:* As children become familiar with their Spanish numbers they can call out the number they spin in Spanish.

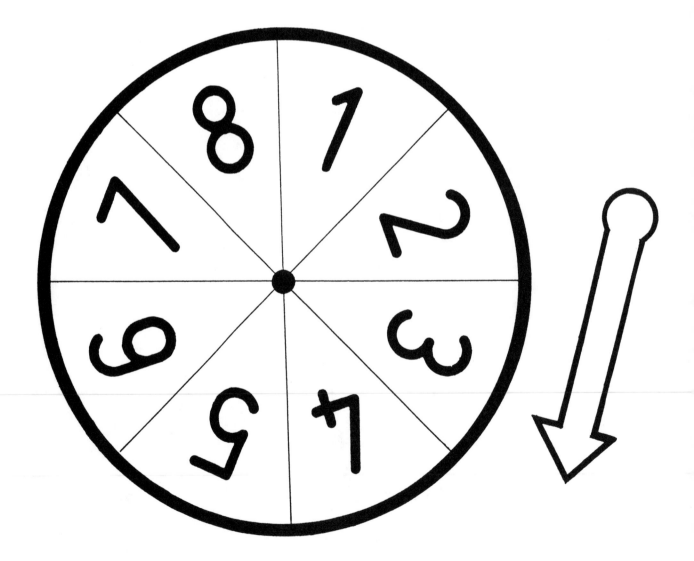

# MY SPANISH PUPPET

Reproduce this page for each child in your class. Have the children color and cut out the puppet parts. Attach with brads. Let the puppets tell you the names of all it's body parts in Spanish.

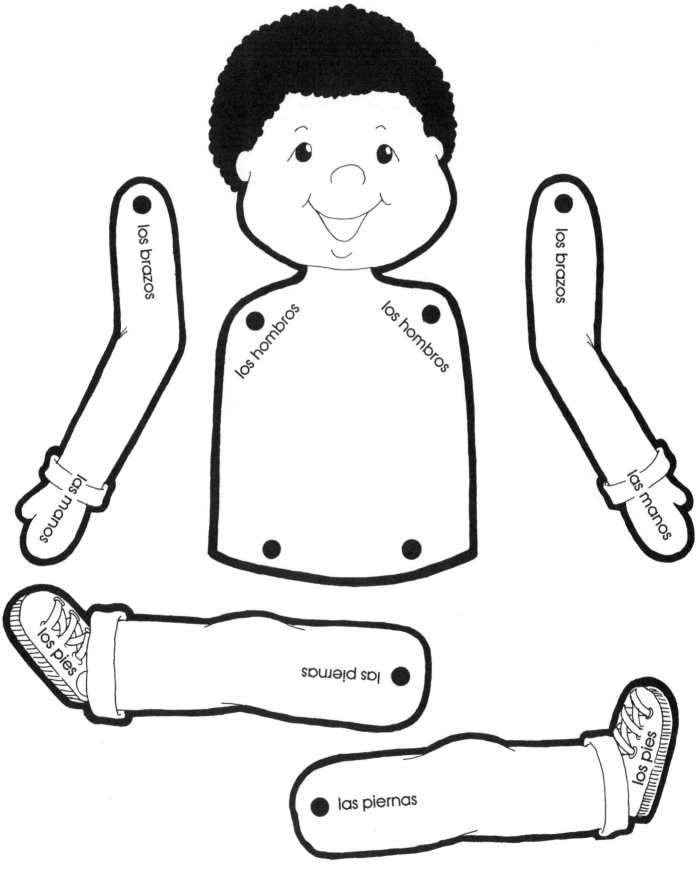

NAME —————————————

When the children appear to have a solid comprehension of the new vocabulary in the "Parts of the Body" unit, have them color the picture below to place in their Spanish workbook.

## I KNOW MY BODY PARTS IN SPANISH
### DATE ———————————

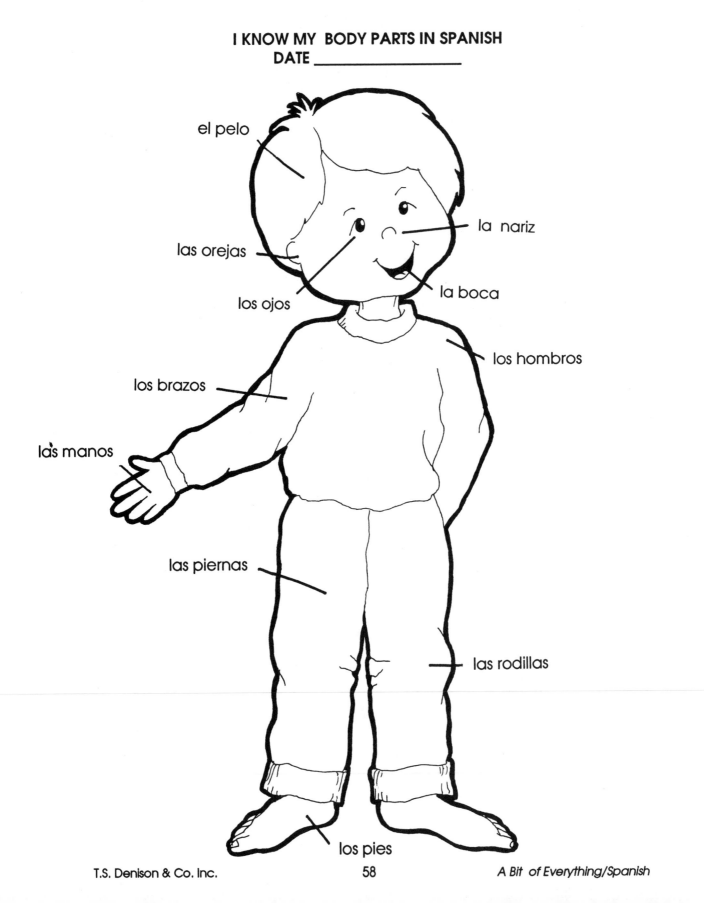

el pelo

la nariz

las orejas

la boca

los ojos

los hombros

los brazos

las manos

las piernas

las rodillas

los pies

# FELT BOARD DRESS UP PATTERNS

hat
el sombrero

sweater
el suéter

pants
los pantalones

dress
el vestido

tie
la corbata

shorts
los pantalones cortos

# GIRL AND BOY DRESS-UP CHARACTERS

## DRESS UP BOX

The ever-popular dress up box in your class can become a completely new and exciting experience for your students. Add some new clothing to the box and label it with the new Spanish vocabulary. Then allow children to use the articles of clothing as they would on any other given day, but require that they use their new Spanish vocabulary while they role play.

## "SEÑORA/SEÑOR MAY I"

Many people remember the familiar game "Mother May I?" This game is quite similar and is a great tool to ingrain the new vocabulary for this unit. Choose one child to be the "Señora." Have all the other children line up across the room facing the Señora. The Señora must face away from the children. While doing this the children quietly ask if they may take a certain number of steps forwards. "Señora" can not look at the children but can respond by saying a "If you are wearing a _____ then you may take _____ steps forward." The blanks must be filled with a Spanish vocabulary word for a particular article of clothing and a randomly chosen number of steps for the classmate(s) to take forward – in Spanish, of course! Those children wearing that article called out by the "Señora" may move forward the number of steps indicated. The first child to reach the "Señora" may assume her/his role as the Señora (or Señor if the child is a male).

Color the articles of clothing below. Then with a friend, discuss when you would wear each particular article of clothing. Remember to only use your Spanish vocabulary. If you can recall vocabulary from other units try to use it as well.

shoes
los zapatos

sweater
el suéter

hat
el sombrero

dress
el vestido

shirt
la camisa

socks
los calcetines

jacket
la chaqueta

tie
la corbata

pants
los pantalones

shorts
los pantalones cortos

# UNIT 8

# FOODS

## VOCABULARY

|  |  | (pronunciation) |
| --- | --- | --- |
| milk | la leche | *lah leh-cheh* |
| water | el agua | *el ah-gwah* |
| bread | el pan | *el pahn* |
| ice cream | el helado | *el eh-lah-doe* |
| grapes | las uvas | *lahs oo-bahs* |
| apple | la manzana | *lah mahn-sah-nah* |
| orange | la naranja | *lah nah-rahn-ghah* |
| banana | el plátano | *el <u>plah</u>-tah-no* |
| cake | el pastel | *el pahs-<u>tell</u>* |
| butter | la mantequilla | *lah man-teh-kee-yah* |
| egg | el huevo | *el wheh-boh* |
| chicken | el pollo | *el poh-yo* |
| cereal | el cereal | *el seh-reh-<u>ahl</u>* |
| salad | la ensalada | *lah en-sah-lah-dah* |
| hamburger | la hamburguesa | *lah ahm-buhr-gay-sah* |
| chocolate | el chocolate | *el choh-koh-lah-teh* |
| candy | los dulces | *lohs dool-sehs* |
| strawberry | la fresa | *lah freh-sah* |
| potato | la patata | *lah pah-tah-tah* |
| carrot | la zanahoria | *lah sah-nah-<u>or</u>-ee-yah* |

# FOOD PATTERNS

Use the cut out patterns from page 70 through 72 to make replicas of favorite foods. These patterns can be used for felt boards, or can be cut out of a heavier card stock for game use.

bread
el pan

hamburger
la hamburguesa

carrot
la zanahoria

chocolate
el chocolate

potato
la patata

candy
los dulces

# FOOD PATTERNS

cereal
el cereal

cake
el pastel

water
el agua

banana
el plátano

salad
la ensalada

grapes
las uvas

# FOOD PATTERNS

strawberry
la fresa

chicken
el pollo

orange
la naranja

ice cream
el helado

butter
la mantequilla

egg
el huevo

apple
la manzana

## SPANISH MENU GAMES

Using the food patterns from the previous pages, have the children design menus for a Spanish restaurant. They must put all the names of the food on the menu (younger children could draw pictures instead of writing the words). When the menus have been designed, set up a role play stage. For the first time, set up a table with place settings for four people. Then choose four children who have confidence with their new Spanish vocabulary. Have one person be the waiter/waitress who takes the orders. Orders must be placed using the Spanish food vocabulary.

## SPANISH LUNCH DAY

Have all the children bring a lunch to school. Set up a picnic environment in the classroom or outdoors. Have each child take turns telling what they have in their lunch using as much of their Spanish food vocabulary as possible. A Spanish dictionary may be very helpful to you! Children will likely ask if you know vocabulary for other items in their lunches. Buen Provecho (Eat Well)!

# A SPANISH/MEXICAN FAVORITE

## Taco ingredients:

1 dozen corn tortillas
vegetable oil for frying
2 cups ground, cooked meat
shredded lettuce, chopped tomatoes, grated cheddar or jack cheese
bottled salsa

## Directions:

1.  Heat oil and fry tortilla lightly on one side. Turn over with tongs, and fold in half. Fry both sides until lightly crisp.

2.  Drain on paper towels, continue with remaining tortillas.

3.  Fill taco shells with meat and desired condiments.

4.  Beans, peppers, and onion are excellent additions as well.

Serves 4

# FOOD BINGO GAME

Copy the cards provided to make enough copies so that each child in the class has at least one card. Use whatever markers you have available (dots, beans, popcorn kernels, etc.). Place the cut-out patterns from the first page of this unit in a bag. Then draw the food from the bag to start the game. The first child to cover a line of three wins the game. Remember to use only Spanish vocabulary for the foods. Allow different children the opportunity to draw the food cards from the bag.

# FOOD BINGO

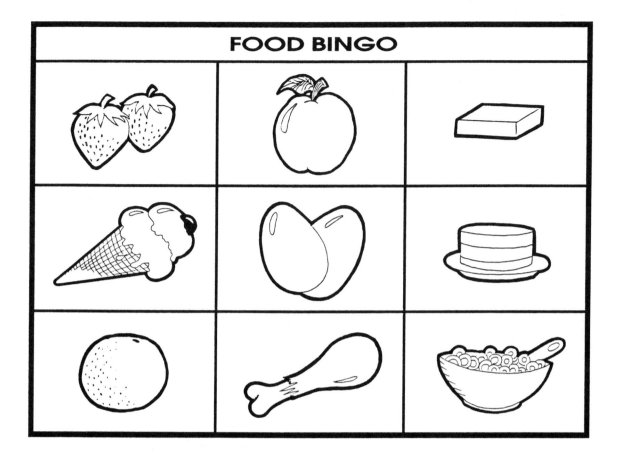

# FOOD BINGO

# FOOD BINGO

# FOOD BINGO

## PREPARE A MEAL

Have the children cut out pictures of food from magazines. Ask the children to plan a meal using the pictures of food they have found. Glue the pictures on the plate. Can the children name the foods using their Spanish vocabulary.

Color all the foods that you can remember from the Spanish Food Unit. If there **FUN SHEET**
is a food you have forgotten, ask a friend for help.

# UNIT 7

# ARTICLES OF CLOTHING

## VOCABULARY

|  |  | *(pronunciation)* |
|---|---|---|
| shirt | la camisa | *lah- kah-mee-sah* |
| pants | los pantalones | *lohs  pahn-tah-loh-nehs* |
| dress | el vestido | *el bes-tee-doe* |
| shorts | los pantalones cortos | *lohs pahn-tah-loh-nehs kor-tohs* |
| sweater | el suéter | *el sweh-tehr* |
| socks | los calcetines | *lohs kahl-seh-teen-ehs* |
| shoes | los zapatos | *lohs sah-pah-tohs* |
| hat | el sombrero | *el  sohm-breh-roh* |
| jacket | la chaqueta | *lah  chah-keh-tah* |
| tie | la corbata | *lah kor-bah-tah* |

# FELT BOARD DRESS UP PATTERNS

Learning the Spanish vocabulary for articles of clothing comes naturally when it is a daily routine topic. The following three pages will provide you with the clothing patterns and the girl and boy felt board characters. Leave the characters and the clothing options up on a felt board and allow students to dress them on their own. Be certain that students are first introduced to the Spanish vocabulary for this unit and that they remember to use it when they are playing with the girl and boy cut-outs during their free time. These patterns can also be used for group activities. Children can take turns dressing the character cut-outs while reciting his articles of clothing in Spanish! *(Let the children in your class give the characters Spanish names.)*

shirt
la camisa

jacket
la chaqueta

shoes
los zapatos

socks
los calcetines

# UNIT 9
# ANIMALS

## VOCABULARY

| | | (pronunciation) |
|---|---|---|
| cat | el gato | *el gah-toe* |
| dog | el perro | *el peh-roh* |
| cow | la vaca | *lah-bah-kah* |
| horse | el caballo | *el kah-bah-yo* |
| chicken | la gallina | *lah gah-yee-nah* |
| pig | el puerco | *el pwehr-koh* |
| sheep | la oveja | *lah oh-beh-ghah* |
| bird | el pájaro | *el <u>pa</u>-ghah-ro* |
| bear | el oso | *el oh-so* |
| snake | la culebra | *lah koo-leh-brah* |

# ANIMAL PATTERNS

Patterns for cut-outs of animals are found on pages 84 & 85. Each animal is labeled with the appropriate Spanish vocabulary. Introduce the children to the new vocabulary and arrange the animals for a bulletin board display.

bird
el pájaro

chicken
la gallina

sheep
la oveja

cow
la vaca

snake
la culebra

# ANIMAL PATTERNS

cat
el gata

bear
el oso

pig
el puerco

horse
el caballo

dog
el perro

## WHO'S ZOO?

Have each child bring a stuffed animal from home. Designate a corner of your room for the *Who's Zoo*. Have each child display their stuffed animal in that corner. Have each child introduce their animal using first the English name they chose for their pretend pet, and then what type of animal it is using the new Spanish vocabulary word. (Example: "Hi, this is Fluffy. He is el perro")

## ANIMAL SOUNDS

Old MacDonald is an all-time favorite song that can be used for reinforcing the Spanish vocabulary for different animals. Try the combinations below using the old familiar tune.

| And on his farm he had . . . a | with a . . . |
|---|---|
| el perro | bark, bark, here |
| el gato | meow, meow, here |
| el caballo | nah, nah, here |
| la vaca | moo, moo, here |
| la culebra | sss, sss, here |

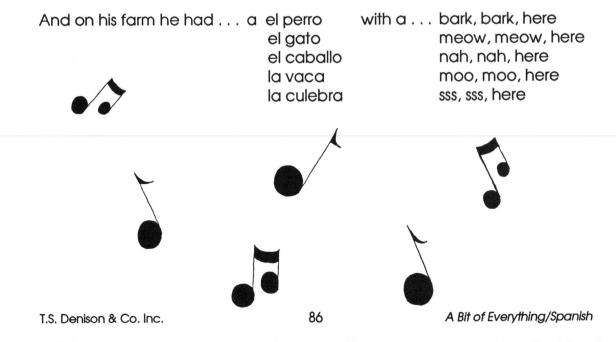

# ANIMAL PUPPETS

Give each of the children a lunch-size paper bag, construction paper and a variety of different colored scrap paper. Using the paper, let the children create a paper bag puppet. Each child should know the animal's name in Spanish. When the puppets are complete, let the children put on a puppet show with their Spanish animal. It is also fun to sing *Old MacDonald Had A Farm*, singing the animal's names in Spanish.

# ANIMAL MATCHING

Draw a line from the adult animal on the left to the baby animal on the right.
Can you say the name of the animal in Spanish?

# UNIT 10
# FAMILY MEMBERS

## VOCABULARY

| | | (pronounciation) |
|---|---|---|
| mother | la madre | lah ma-dreh |
| father | el padre | el pa-dreh |
| sister | la hermana | lah ehr-ma-nah |
| brother | el hermano | el ehr-ma-no |
| grandmother | la abuela | lah ah-bweh-lah |
| grandfather | el abuelo | el ah-bweh-lo |
| aunt | la tía | lah tee-yah |
| uncle | el tío | el tee-yo |
| cousin | (masculine) el primo | el pree-mo |
| | (feminine) la prima | lah pree-mah |
| cat | el gato | el gah-toe |
| dog | el perro | el peh-roh |
| baby | el bebé | el  beh-_beh_ |

# PATTERNS FOR FAMILY MEMBERS

Use the patterns below and on page 93 for cut outs to introduce the new "family members" vocabulary. Allow children to arrange them on either a felt board or bulletin board. Remember to keep the display boards at a level low enough so that the children can Spanish role play on their own.

baby
el bebé

sister
la hermana

grandmother
la abuela

grandfather
el abuelo

# PATTERNS FOR FAMILY MEMBERS

brother
el hermano

father
el padre

mother
la madre

# STORY TIME

Read a familiar story like, "The Three Bears," using the Spanish vocabulary for the family members. Then have the children retell the story from memory using the new vocabulary and any other unit vocabulary they may recall. Storytime might easily become a language experience as well. On a large piece of paper, use bold print to write the story being retold by the children. Highlight the new Spanish vocabulary using a different colored marker. Finally, after the story is complete, have the children assist you in rereading what you have written.

# PICTURE DAY

Have each child bring a picture of his/her family. Encourage the children to bring a photograph that includes their extended family if possible. Have each child take a turn showing their photograph and introducing the members of their family using the vocabulary from this unit. As an extension to this activity, make a bulletin board display that is in the form of a tree. Stick each child's photograph on the tree and label the pictures with child's first name (Erick's family, etc.).

Color the people below. Draw a line to match the picture with the Spanish
word for the person.

**la madre**

**el padre**

**el   hermano**

**la hermana**

**el bebé**

# UNIT 11

# MODES OF TRANSPORTATION

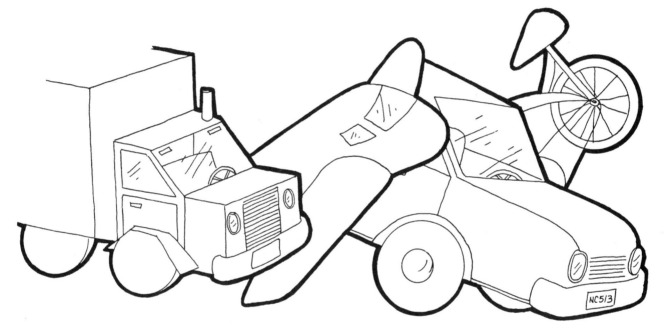

## VOCABULARY

| | | (prounciation) |
|---|---|---|
| car | el carro | el kah-roh |
| bus | el autobús | el ah-oo-toe-_boos_ |
| truck | el camión | el kah-mee-_yohn_ |
| bike | la bicicleta | la bee-see-kleh-tah |
| boat | el barco | el bahr-ko |
| plane | el avión | el ah-byohn |
| ski | el esquí | el eh-_skee_ |
| helicopter | el helicóptero | el eh-lee-kop-teh-ro |
| air balloon | el globo | el gloh-bo |
| scooter | el patinete | el pah-tee-neh-teh |

# MODES OF TRANSPORTATION

Collect a large box of magazines. Have children cut out pictures which show various modes of transportation (remember to define "transportation" to the younger children). Then have the children glue the pictures on a large board in collage form. When the collage is complete, have a group discussion and introduce the children to the Spanish vocabulary for modes of transportation. Display the collage in the classroom for the remainder of the unit.

# INDEPENDENTLY CREATIVE TRANSPORTATION

Give the children a period of uninterrupted time to use legos or building blocks of some sort to build a vehicle. Try to keep the children working independently or in very small groups, this will encourage individual creativity. Finally, allow children to share their masterpieces in front of the class. Remember to have children use their Spanish vocabulary in their introductions.

NAME _____ # TRANSPORTATION

**FUN SHEET**

Color the picture of the different forms of transportation below. Practice the new vocabulary before finding a friend to review the words. After reviewing the words, take turns telling your friend how you would use each mode of transportation. For example: " I would use *el barco* to travel over water or go water skiing."

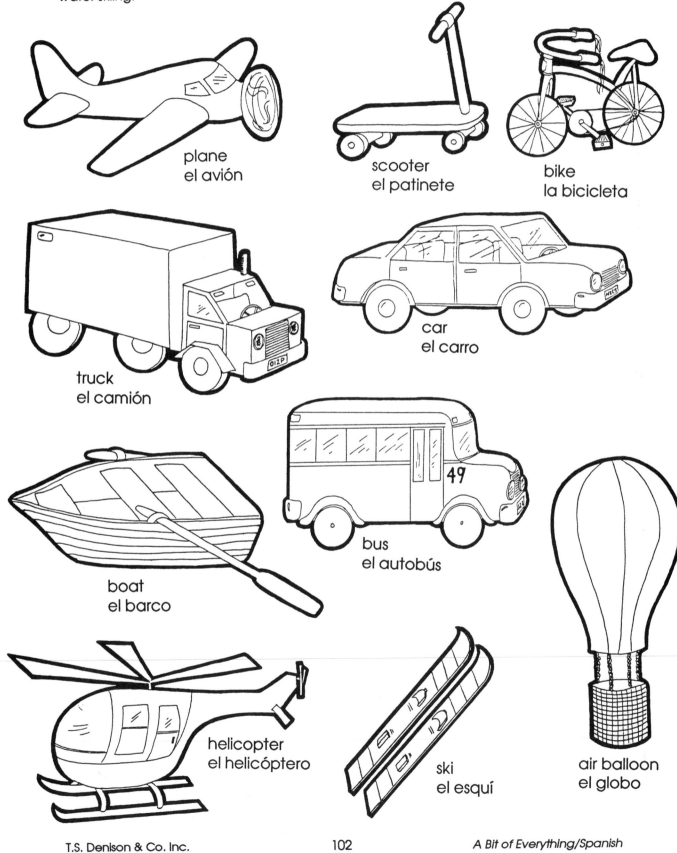

plane
el avión

scooter
el patinete

bike
la bicicleta

truck
el camión

car
el carro

boat
el barco

bus
el autobús

helicopter
el helicóptero

ski
el esquí

air balloon
el globo

# UNIT 12

# SPECIAL PLACES

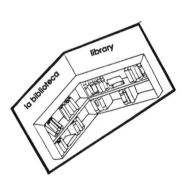

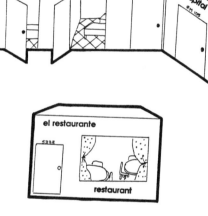

## VOCABULARY

| | | (pronunciation) |
|---|---|---|
| house | la casa | *lah kah-sah* |
| kitchen | la cocina | *lah koh-see-nah* |
| bedroom | el dormitorio | *el door-mee-tohr-yo* |
| school | la escuela | *lah eh-skweh-lah* |
| library | la biblioteca | *lah bee-blee-yoh-teh-kah* |
| hospital | el hospital | *el oh-spee-tahl* |
| church | la iglesia | *lah ee-gleh-syah* |
| restaurant | el restaurante | *el reh-stahw-rahn-teh* |
| bakery | la panadería | *lah pah-nah-dah-ree-ya* |
| bank | el banco | *el bahn-ko* |

# SPECIAL PLACES

Introduce your class to two new vocabulary words each day by simulating two different role play areas in your classroom. Some of the places will need little or no effort to establish (like the role play area for the word "school"). Divide the class in half and allow the children to have free time playing in each area. Do this for 15 minutes a day for one week to reinforce the new vocabulary.

# SPECIAL PLACES MATCHING GAME PATTERNS

Copy the patterns on pages 106 through 109. Have children match the objects with the room or place to which it belongs. For example: "The book comes from the biblioteca." Allow the children to lead the group, reminding them to only use the new Spanish vocabulary from this unit.

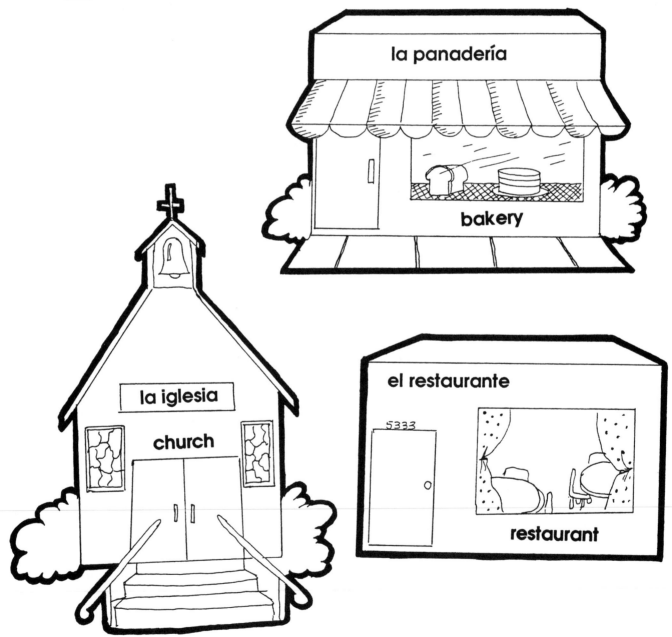

# SPECIAL PLACES MATCHING GAME PATTERNS

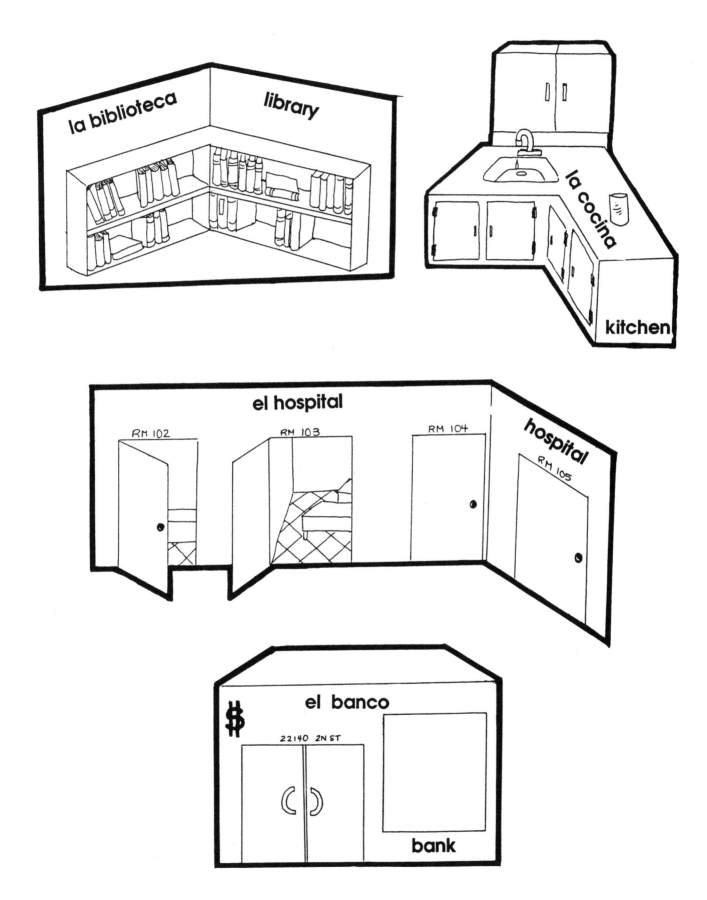

la biblioteca

library

la cocina

kitchen

el hospital

RM 102

RM 103

RM 104

hospital

RM 105

el banco

$

22140 2N ST

bank

# SPECIAL PLACES MATCHING GAME PATTERNS

bedroom

el dormitorio

5 UNITED STATES OF AMERICA D3211 9805B

D321198 05B 5

la escuela

school

la casa

house

# SPECIAL PLACES MATCHING GAME PATTERNS

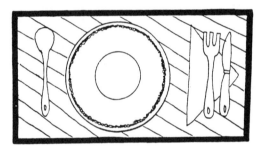

# SPECIAL PLACES

Look at each of the special places. Draw a picture of something that you would find at that special place.

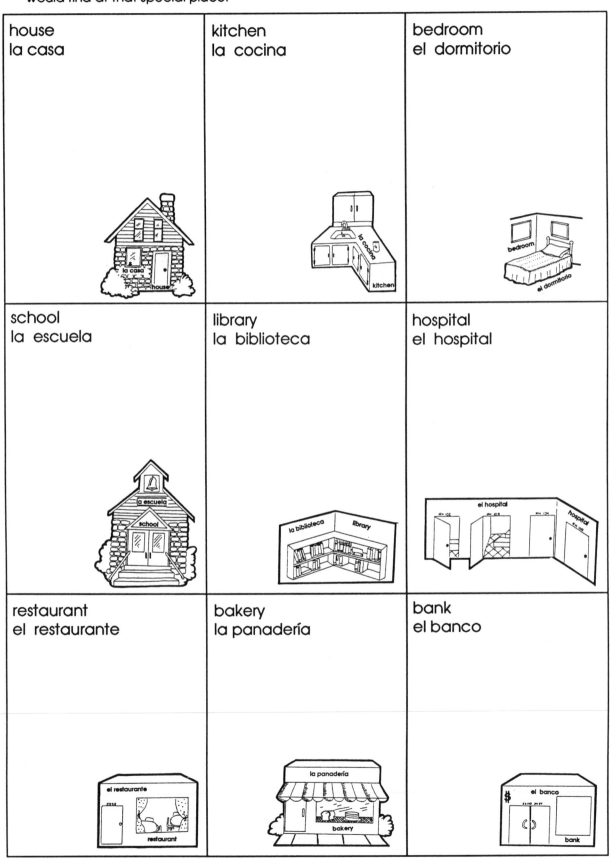

| house la casa | kitchen la cocina | bedroom el dormitorio |
| school la escuela | library la biblioteca | hospital el hospital |
| restaurant el restaurante | bakery la panadería | bank el banco |

# UNIT 13

# COMMON PHRASES

## VOCABULARY

| | | (pronounciation) |
|---|---|---|
| Hello | Hola | oh-lah |
| How are you? | ¿Qué tal? | keh tahl |
| I am fine. | Estoy bien | eh-stoy byehn |
| And you? | ¿Y tú? | ee too |
| Very well | Muy bien. | mwee byehn |
| Thank you | Gracias | grah-see-yahs |
| What time is it? | ¿Qué hora es? | keh oh-rah  ehs |
| It is ___ o'clock | Son las _____ | sohn lahs |
| | Es la una. | ehs  lah oo-nah |

("Es" is used with one o'clock, and "son" is used with all other times.)

| | | |
|---|---|---|
| Good-bye | Adiós | ah-dee-yohs |
| Good night | Buenas noches | bweh-nahs noe-chehs |

# COMMON PHRASES

By making it a routine to begin each Spanish group time using the same greetings, your students will quickly acquire some common Spanish phrases into their vocabulary. Begin by writing down the greetings on a large piece of paper. Have students follow along with the readings for the first couple weeks and slowly remove or cover a portion of the text until all can be recited from memory. Use the paragraph below as a guideline to transfer the phrases to a large poster-sized board.

| | |
|---|---|
| *Reader:* | Hola. ¿Qué tal? |
| *Students:* | Estoy bien. ¿Y tú? |
| *Reader:* | Muy bien. Gracias. |
| *Students:* | ¿Qué hora es? |
| *Reader:* | Son las ____. |
| *Students:* | Gracias. Adiós. |
| *Reader:* | Buenas noches. |

# THE MEXICAN FLAG

# THE SPANISH FLAG

# MAP OF MEXICO

Draw in some of the things that you think you might see in Mexico.

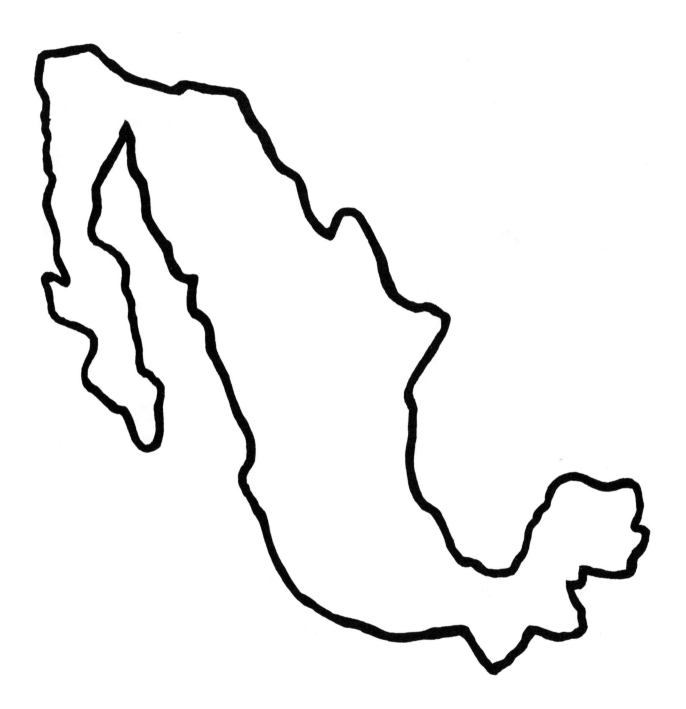

# MAP OF SPAIN

Draw in some of the things that you think you might see in Spain.

# (Un Poco De Todo)

## Games, Activities, and Cue Cards
## for Introducing Spanish
## to Young Children

*A Bit of Everything/Spanish* is translated from the book
*A Bit of Everything/French* written by
Liza Sernett

Spanish translation by
Monica Kenton Morales

illustrations by
Liza Sernett

*Publishers*
T.S. Denison and Company, Inc.
Minneapolis, Minnesota 55431

## T.S. Denison & Co., Inc.

"Materials designed by teachers, for teachers" is a statement that the T.S. Denison Company is extremely proud of. All of our quality educational products are tried, tested, and proven effective—by teachers!

For over 100 years, T.S. Denison has been a leader in educational publishing. Thousands of teachers look to us for new and innovative aids to make their work more enjoyable and more rewarding. We are committed to developing and publishing educational materials that will assist teachers in building a strong curriculum for young children.

Plan for great teaching experiences when you use materials from the T.S. Denison Company.

## Dedication

I dedicate this book to all the children at *Starting Space*.
Thank you for teaching me the importance of savoring
one's creativity, sense of humor, and desire to learn!

Standard Book Number: 0-513-02105-1
*A Bit of Everything Spanish (Un Poco De Todo)*
Copyright © 1992 by T.S. Denison & Co., Inc.
Minneapolis, Minnesota 55431

Printed in the USA